OUTBACK

Australia

NEW
HOLLAND

OUTBACK

SHAEN ADEY

JANE BURTON TAYLOR

Australia

NEW
HOLLAND

First published in 1998 by New Holland Publishers Pty Ltd
Sydney • London • Cape Town

Produced and published in Australia by
New Holland Publishers Pty Ltd
3/2 Aquatic Drive, Frenchs Forest
NSW 2086, Australia

24 Nutford Place, London W1H 6DQ
United Kingdom

80 McKenzie Street, Cape Town 8001
South Africa

National Library of Australia Cataloguing-in-Publication Data:

Taylor, Jane Burton.
Outback Australia.

ISBN 1 86436 323 1.

1. Australia – Pictorial works. 2. Australia – Description and travel.

994.0222

Publishing General Manager: Jane Hazell
Publisher: Averill Chase
Concept Design: Trinity Fry
Senior Designer: Lyndall du Toit
Editors: Emma Wise, Anouska Good
DTP Cartographers: John Loubser, Lyndall du Toit
Picture Researcher: Bronwyn Rennex

Reproduction by Hirt and Carter Cape (Pty) Ltd
Printed and bound by Tien Wah Press (Pte) Ltd
in Singapore

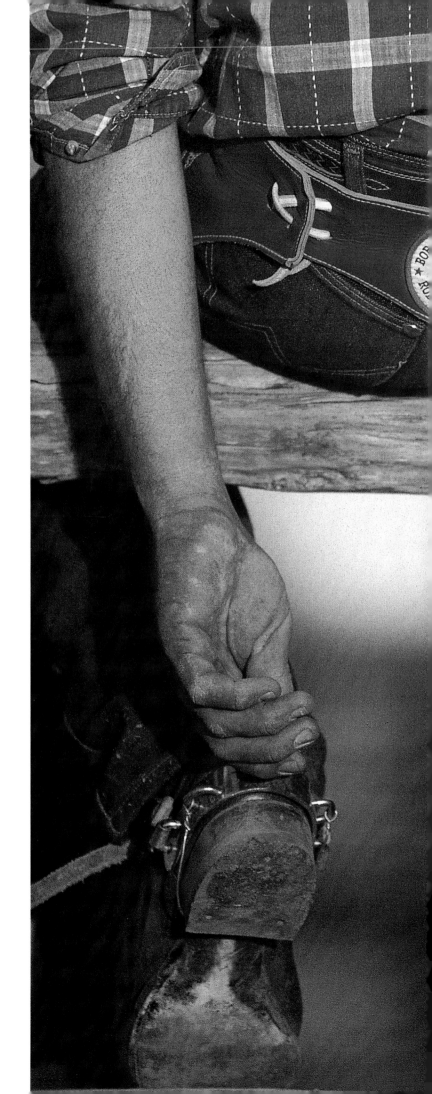

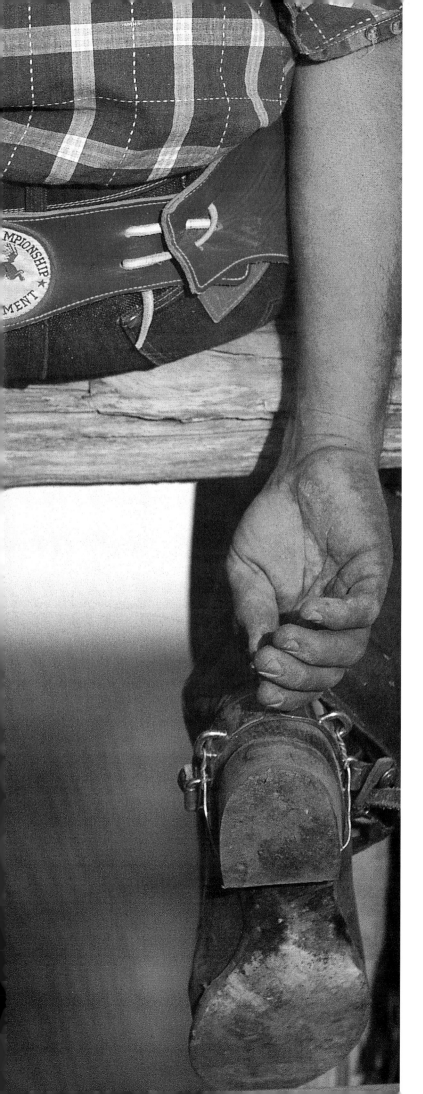

Photographic Acknowledgements

All photographs by **Shaen Adey © New Holland Image Library**
with the exception of the following:

Bill Bachman: endpapers, pp4–5, 12, 26 (bottom),
104–105; **Colin Beard**: pp32–33, 60–61; **Jane Burton Taylor**:
p67 (top); **David Hancock/Skyscans**: p66 (top right);
Anthony Johnson/New Holland Image Library: pp68–69,
109 (top); **Dave Watts/Wild Images**: p91; **Sorrel Wilby &
Chris Ciantar/Wild Side**: pp14, 15, 24 (bottom left).

Endpapers: Mustering cattle by motorbike at sunset.
Half title: Chambers Pillar in the Simpson Desert.
Title page: A lone boab on the road to Kununurra.
Left: Cowboy at the Queen's Birthday Rodeo, Normanton.
Contents page: A deserted railway siding
en route to Alice Springs.

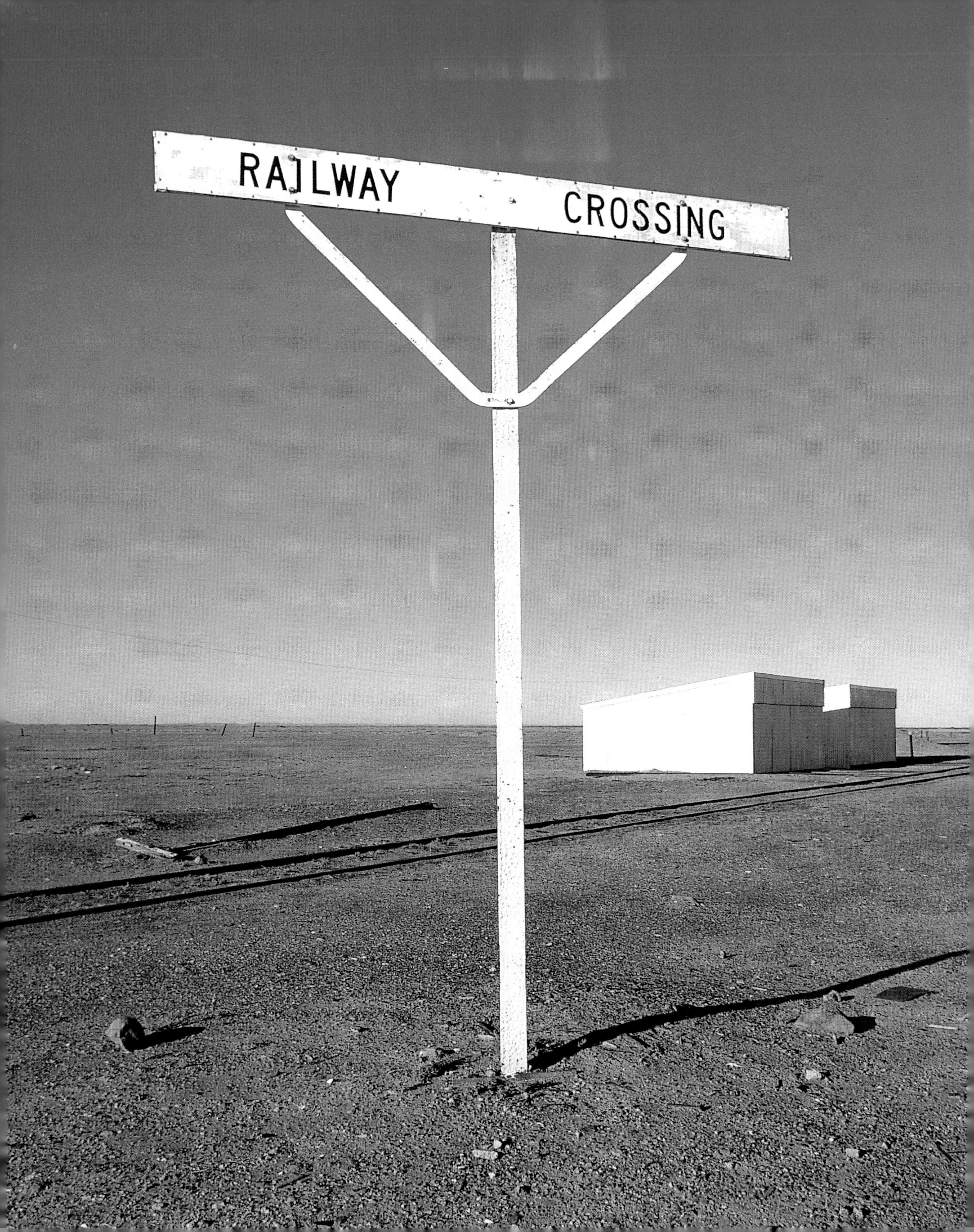
RAILWAY CROSSING

N

Arafura

*Cobourg
Peninsula*

Timor Sea

DARWIN

Litchfield N.P.

Kakadu N.P.

*Arn
Lan*

INDIAN OCEAN

Nitmiluk N.P.

Drysdale
River N.P.

Kununurra

*Lake
Argyle*

*Kimberley
Region*

Purnululu
(Bungle Bungle)
N.P.

Windjana
Gorge N.P.

Derby

Tunnel
Creek N.P.

Broome

Geikie
Gorge N.P.

Halls
Creek

*Bungle Bungle
Range*

Wolfe Creek
Crater N.P.

*TANAMI
DESERT*

Tennant Creek

*GREAT SANDY
DESERT*

Devils Marbles

Port Hedland

Karratha

NORTHER

Millstream–
Chichester N.P.

Karijini N.P.

TERRITOR

GIBSON DESERT

West MacDonnell N.P.

Ningaloo M.P.

Hamersley Range

Newman

Finke Gorge N.P.

S

LITTLE SANDY DESERT

Kings Canyon

R
V

Carnarvon

Shark Bay M.P.

Uluru–
Katatjuta N.P.

MacDonnell Ra

WESTERN AUSTRALIA

*Zuytdorp
Cliffs*

Kalbarri N.P.

*GREAT VICTORIA
DESERT*

SIMPS

Geraldton

Coober P

Nambung N.P.

SOUTI

Broad Arrow

Kalgoorlie–Boulder

NULLARBOR PLAIN

Nullarbor R.R.

Northam

PERTH

Fremantle

Wave Rock

Norseman

Eucla

Ce

Bunbury

Fitzgerald
River N.P.

Esperance

Great

Cape Le
Grand N.P.

Australian   Bight

Albany

SOUTHERN   OCEAN

Torres Strait

Cape York
Jardine River N.P.

Weipa
Iron Range N.P.

Northern Reef

Mungkan Kandju N.P.

Gulf of Carpentaria

Coral Sea

Cape York Peninsula

Lakefield N.P.
Cooktown

Daintree N.P.
Cairns

SOUTH PACIFIC OCEAN

Great Barrier Reef

Atherton Tableland

Central Reef – Whitsunday Passage

Lawn Hill N.P.

Gulf Savannah

Townsville

Charters Towers

Whitsunday Is. N.P.

Cloncurry
Porcupine Gorge N.P.

Mount Isa

Mackay

Southern Reef – Capricorn Channel

Diamantina Gates N.P.

Longreach

Rockhampton
Gladstone

QUEENSLAND

Carnarvon Gorge N.P.

SIMPSON DESERT

Bundaberg
Fraser Island

Hellhole N.P.

Poeppel Corner
Birdsville

Channel Country

Maryborough

Dalhousie Ruins
Simpson Desert R.R.

STURTS STONY DESERT

nadatta
Innamincka R.R.

Lake Bindegolly N.P.

Toowoomba
BRISBANE

ke Eyre N.P.

Coolangatta

Eyre

STRZELECKI DESERT

Cameron Corner

Lismore

Sturt N.P.

USTRALIA

Gammon Ranges N.P.

Bourke

Grafton

Dorrigo N.P.
Coffs Harbour

Woomera

Mootwingee N.P.
White Cliffs

Pilliga N.P.

Flinders Ranges N.P.

Warrumbungle N.P.

Port Macquarie

Wilpena Pound

Broken Hill

NEW SOUTH WALES

rt Augusta

Kinchega N.P.

Wollemi N.P.

Newcastle

Flinders Ranges

Willandra N.P.

Blue Mtns N.P.

Mungo N.P.

SYDNEY

t Lincoln

Mildura

CANBERRA
A.C.T.

Wollongong

ADELAIDE

Swan Hill

N.P.

Wyperfeld N.P.

Kosciuszko N.P.

Kangaroo Island

VICTORIA

Alpine N.P.

Grampians (Gariwerd)N.P.

MELBOURNE

Portland

Wilsons Promontory N.P.

Tasman Sea

Bass Strait

King Island

Flinders Island

Devonport
Launceston

Cradle Mtn– Lake St Clair N.P.

Franklin–Gordon Wild Rivers N.P.

TASMANIA

Southwest N.P.
HOBART

INTRODUCTION

The Australian outback is one of the last great wild places on earth. Its huge skies, vibrant colours, stark emptiness and startling landscapes are hypnotic. It is a place of grand scale, where roads run ruler-straight across vast desolate plains to treeless horizons, crusty mountain ranges turn mauve in the magic light of dusk, and mysterious ancient landforms are framed by thousands of miles of desert.

A typical outback vista is a vast cloudless blue sky over a rust-red plain half-covered in sage-green spinifex and the sensuous stark white limbs of ghost gums. But the Australian outback encompasses a far greater and more diverse range of landscapes than this. Running from the western foothills of the Great Dividing Range and covering most of the country to the north, west and south coasts – bar heavily cultivated farmlands and pockets of civilisation – it is an expanse that contains some of the most challenging and dramatically beautiful lands on earth.

There can be a mesmerising sameness when driving through outback landscape hour after hour, but there are spectacular landforms too: the rugged wilderness of the sandstone Arnhem Land escarpment; the palm-fringed freshwater gorges of Lawn Hill in Queensland; the beehive domes of the Bungle Bungles; the enigmatic rock outcrops of Uluru and Katatjuta; the ragged backbone of the MacDonnell Ranges cutting across the arid centre of the country; the vivid green wetlands of Kakadu; and the desolate expanse of the Nullarbor Plain.

Like any truly wild place, the Australian outback acts like a magnet: Australians of all ages travel to the outback to rejuvenate themselves in this sparsely populated domain. They cross gruelling tracks on four-wheel-drive adventures and trek along time-worn watercourses to swim in pristine waterholes. They visit ancient rock art sites and camp under night skies crowded with stars, falling asleep in the immense silence of the outback, a silence interrupted only by the night-time thump of a kangaroo moving through the bush or the eerie howl of the dingo just before dawn.

DEFINING THE OUTBACK

Physically the outback is not defined by any set boundaries, although the original word 'outback' may come from the expression 'out back of Bourke'. Bourke, in the central north of New South Wales, is well on the way to the arid terrain fringing the dry desert heart of the Australian continent, the land that is most typically conjured up in the mind's eye as the quintessential outback.

Australia is one of the most stable landmasses in the world and also geologically one of the oldest. For the past 100 million years, the continent has been free of the mountain-building forces that continue to form mountain ranges in other parts of the world. In Australia, the mountains are so 'old' they have eroded to a shadow of their original height.

The country's main watershed is the Great Dividing Range which parallels the east coast for almost the full length of the continent. Rivers run either west or east of these once-towering mountains, which roughly delineate the start of the outback.

To the west of the Great Divide the country flattens out, becoming increasingly dry and desolate toward the centre. Supporting little vegetation and apparently waterless, this central lowland is dotted with salt lakes and distinct landforms such as the dramatic Uluru – the largest monolith on earth. When the desert is flooded briefly by summer rains it is renowned for bursting into life with wildflowers. This region is otherwise watered by a network of over 7000 artesian wells that tap into a gigantic underground aquifer. Scientists say rainwater that falls in the Great Divide travels very slowly across the aquifer – a few centimetres a year – taking an

Opposite Vibrant red dunes stretch as far as the eye can see along the French Line in the Simpson Desert.

11

estimated 1 to 1.5 million years to reach the artesian basin. One thinly populated third of Australia lies north of the Tropic of Capricorn, with Kakadu and much of Arnhem Land and Cape York falling within the monsoonal belt. To the west is a broad plateau that covers two-thirds of the continent and incorporates Australia's largest deserts and the region known as the 'red centre'.

There are also three ancient plateaus – Arnhem Land in the Northern Territory and, fringing the coast of Western Australia, the ruggedly beautiful Kimberley and Pilbara regions with startling formations such as the Bungle Bungles.

THE PEOPLE OF THE OUTBACK

With its sparse and scattered population, the outback is dominated by sprawling sheep and cattle stations that, depending on the quality of the land, can range from 400 to 400 000 hectares. The men and women who own these stations, and those who work as station managers and stockmen, are a breed unto themselves. They live for the most part isolated from mainstream culture, often over a day's drive from the nearest outpost of civilisation. In addition to this extraordinary distance, they are cut off, sometimes for months, when roads are flooded or made impassable by the summer rains, known in the north as the Wet.

Distances in outback Australia are so enormous that many stations receive their mail by plane, and shopping for clothes is often done via mail-order catalogues. Children are linked via high-frequency radio to the School of the Air, and the Royal Flying Doctor Service provides most stations and isolated communities with a regular and emergency medical service. It is a hard and somewhat remarkable lifestyle, one that has created a resilient and idiosyncratic breed of Australians.

Understandably the people of the outback have a strong sense of independence and a resourcefulness that enables them to endure and enjoy a harsh and isolated existence. They are renowned for inventing unusual solutions to gnarly problems and for their irreverent sense of humour, as demonstrated in the annual Henley-on-Todd – a parody of an English regatta held in the dry and dusty riverbed of Alice Springs' Todd River. This event also typifies the propensity the people of the outback have for entertaining themselves. They turn out in huge numbers for sports carnivals, horse races, country dances and rodeos, and take great joy in what outback locals call 'galah sessions' – long chats on the radio with friends and 'near' neighbours who usually live some hundreds of kilometres away.

Bound together in their isolation, the people of the outback enjoy the support of close-knit families and communities.

BELOW On most outback stations the arrival of the mail plane is an event. In the harsh red desert country of Tanami Downs, the mail comes fortnightly and the children wouldn't miss it for anything. For people living on remote stations, it is a crucial link to the world.

Whether working on outback stations or living in isolated settlements or towns, they look out for one another and are always ready to lend a helping hand.

THE ULTIMATE SURVIVORS

A common link between all people of the Australian bush is their great love of the outback, and this is particularly true for Aboriginal people – the original inhabitants of the continent. Aboriginal links with the land stretch back at least 50 000 years; they are the ultimate outback survivors.

Australian Aboriginal culture is the oldest surviving indigenous culture in the world. The Aborigines' immense knowledge of the land has been honed over thousands of generations. While the early white settlers tried to 'conquer' the outback, the Aborigines lived in harmony with it. They survived by developing an intimate knowledge of the seasons, of patterns of wind, rain and sun, and of the animals and plants of their land. All of this knowledge, an intricate system of survival – where to find food, water and medicine – they carefully passed down through the generations.

Traditionally, the desert Aborigines were nomadic and had an annual foraging pattern. They would travel over large tracts of land after rain and retreat to permanent waterholes during the Dry. The men hunted with boomerangs, spears, fishing nets and traps. The women dug for roots and insects such as witchetty grubs and honey ants. They collected other bush foods too – berries, leaves, fruit, and flowers such as waterlilies.

Living in extended family groups, or clans, the Aborigines have a complex social and religious system which is intimately bound to the land. They believe in a creation time, generally known as the Dreamtime. This was the time when Aboriginal

ABOVE This Aboriginal woman is a member of the Amoonguna community, a settlement located 14 kilometres to the south-east of Alice Springs, in Australia's 'red centre'.

spirit ancestors walked the earth and created all the features – trees, animals and landforms – that exist in the outback today.

Although fishermen from Macassar in the Celebes visited Aborigines along the Arnhem Land coast for two centuries prior to the arrival of Captain James Cook, their impact on indigenous culture remained subtle and isolated. The influence of British colonisation was far more profound and widespread – it had an impact on Aboriginal culture that would completely change indigenous life forever.

There was no recognition of the Aborigines' right to the land, in fact Australia was declared *terra nullius* – unoccupied. Many indigenous people died after contracting European diseases to which they had no resistance, others were either killed in battles with early settlers or were literally hunted like wild animals. Missionaries were also active in destroying indigenous culture, travelling to the remotest parts of the country and setting about converting Aboriginal people to Christianity. There was a widespread belief that Aborigines were a dying breed and government policies reflected this. Many thousands of children of mixed parentage were taken from their mothers and adopted into white families or placed in orphanages.

The past few decades have seen the dismantling of such government policies. More recently, a political commitment to reconciliation has acknowledged and attempted to redress the personal and cultural damage done to Aboriginal people.

Today it is in the farthest flung corners of the country – regions isolated by geography and climate such as the Kimberley and Arnhem Land – that the rich culture of Australia's Aboriginal people survives most strongly. The indigenous culture is also alive and well in the desert heart of the continent, where responsibility for the management of the

ABOVE An Aboriginal ranger shows visitors to Uluru how to light a fire in the traditional way, using dry grass to catch the sparks generated by rubbing two sticks together. The Uluru–Katatjuta National Park is jointly managed by indigenous and non-indigenous rangers.

1788, the Blue Mountains defied all explorers' attempts to cross them. Finally, with pressure mounting to find new lands to support the burgeoning colony, three landowners – Blaxland, Lawson and Wentworth – followed the ridgelines and succeeded in crossing the mountains in 1813. Once the fertile grazing plains to the west of the mountain range were opened up, it took only two years before a road was constructed as far as the present town of Bathurst.

Slowly the inland was unlocked by a string of courageous individuals. Early explorers were driven by the dream of an inland sea, a potential source of much-needed fresh water on one of the driest continents on earth. The explorers did not find an inland sea but they did succeed in forging passages across the continent. They were hailed as heroes, even if their explorations ended in failure. In 1862, John McDouall Stuart, on his third gruelling attempt, reached the coast near Port Darwin, establishing an overland link between the north and south coasts. This discovery of an all-weather route from Adelaide to the north paved the passage for the Overland Telegraph Line, completed in 1872. The various telegraph stations along the route provided safe departure points for other pioneers, enabling further exploration of inland Australia.

Uluru–Katatjuta National Park, now returned to its traditional owners, is shared by the local Anangu community and both Aboriginal and white rangers.

Aboriginal culture is now undergoing something of a rebirth in the outback. With the returning of traditional lands, many Aboriginal people are becoming increasingly involved in tourism – taking people through their country, showing them rock art sites, bush food and medicine. This is just one of many types of enterprises springing up around the country which nurture indigenous culture and provide insights for non-Aboriginal people. This new 'indigenous tourism' offers an intriguing opportunity for outsiders to look at the outback 'through Aboriginal eyes'.

After the explorers came a flood of anonymous adventurers. Following the tracks established along Aboriginal trading routes and by the explorers, these early pioneering men and women found promising farmland and settled, leaving the formalities of occupation until later. They took possession by 'squatting' and became the 'squatters' – members of the upper class of the newly born Australian nation.

The gold rushes of the 1850s marked the end of the squatting movement and, together with the search for other valuable gem and mineral deposits, were responsible for opening up new areas of the outback to settlement. Towns sprang up to serve the gold diggings and mining areas and remained to serve surrounding pastoralists. Railways connected towns, gradually replacing the old bullock-drawn drays that carried wool to market, and fences were built in place of the old-style shepherds.

EUROPEAN SETTLEMENT

While non-Aboriginal Australians have had a far shorter relationship with the outback than the Aboriginal people, it has been a major influence in the shaping of the national character.

Ever since Australia's east coast was discovered by Captain Cook in 1770 and subsequently colonised by the British, the outback has called to Europeans seeking adventure. For some years after the founding of a settlement at Port Jackson in

It was the end of an era in the Australian bush, but those early pioneering years succeeded in giving rise to the country's most enduring image of what it means to be an Australian. In the late 19th century the people of the bush – swagmen, shearers and drovers – were celebrated in the rural poetry of Henry Lawson and Banjo Paterson, author of the Australia's informal national anthem, 'Waltzing Matilda'. Artists such as Tom Roberts romanticised bush life with paintings of shearing sheds, bushrangers and drovers wheeling unruly flocks of sheep. Although Australians now see themselves as becoming more sophisticated and cosmopolitan, the outback continues to play a crucial role in the Australian identity.

To early European settlers, the outback was everything the green and pleasant land of their birth was not, yet they made it their home. The outback ethos was born of this struggle to make the wide and often harsh Australian continent their own. A vast and ancient domain, it remains a rugged place where people can experience the stillness of wilderness and wonder at its great and ancient beauty.

SCHOOL OF THE AIR

One of the hardships of life in the outback in the early days was the lack of access to basic infrastructure such as schooling. Until comparatively recently, the main option for children of the outback was to attend boarding school. In 1944, this changed when Adelaide Meithke recognised the potential of using the Royal Flying Doctor Service's radio facilities for linking up children on isolated stations with school teachers in major towns or outback centres. Using high frequency radio transceivers, the first School of the Air was launched in Alice Springs in 1951.

Today the Alice Springs School of the Air has its own radio frequency and there are 13 other schools of the air dotted across the Australian outback. Alice Springs teaches from preschool through primary and broadcasts to an area of 1.3 million square kilometres, with the furthest student an exceptional 1000 kilometres away.

Originally children were sent correspondence lessons and written work would be returned by mail. Nowadays many children have computers (supplied mostly by the School of the Air) and the use of the Internet is increasingly popular, with children receiving and returning written assignments and communications with their teachers promptly via e-mail.

LEFT Ragged tufts of grass are all that survive in much of the vast arid expanse of the Northern Territory. Clouds in the normally clear blue sky signal the possibility of eagerly awaited rain.

THE EAST

THE EAST
Over the Great Divide

The eastern seaboard is the most densely populated region on the Australian continent. Separating this lush coastal strip from the interior is the Great Dividing Range which presented a natural barrier for early European settlers. But it was not to contain the new arrivals for very long – within 50 years of settlement, the continent's highest mountain range had been crossed and the push into the vast Australian inland had begun.

Today, leaving the coast and driving west, it takes around a day before any telltale signs of the outback appear. Typically the country is increasingly dry, roads are straight and narrow and disappear into a flat horizon where mesmerising water mirages appear, shimmering in the relentless heat. Often mobs of kangaroos can be seen loping alongside the road or across a distant paddock. Out here, towns are few and far between but are a welcome, slow-paced respite. Especially seductive to the weary traveller are the charming old hotels or pubs with deep, shady verandahs – the perfect spot to 'down' a cold beer in true outback tradition.

Over the past 200 years, non-Aboriginal Australians have been drawn to the outback by two things: the desire to run cattle or sheep, and the hope of profiting from gold or other valuable minerals. Today the largest town in outback New South Wales reflects this pursuit of mineral wealth: Broken Hill has a population of some 25 000 and sits atop the world's richest lode of silver, lead and zinc.

Though not the largest outback town in New South Wales, Bourke is probably the best known. In the 1890s the famous Australian bush poet, Henry Lawson, lived in one of Bourke's 22 pubs and it is said the town has changed little since then. Set on the eastern bank of the Darling River, and considered by some to be the unofficial boundary of the outback, Bourke was established as a frontier town. Wool arrived by camel train from remote outlying stations and was loaded onto boats to be taken down the river for export to England.

In this western region of New South Wales, there is also a string of fascinating national parks – Mootwingee, Mungo and Kinchega. Mootwingee is dominated by the gnarled Bynguano Range which shelters some weird and wonderful geological formations and over 300 Aboriginal rock art sites. The Wilyakali people created the art here and used rockpools as their water supply during the severe hot summer months.

Once part of Australia's first sheep station, Kinchega National Park is dominated by sand plains and dunes, with massive river red gums lining the Darling River, the park's eastern boundary. World Heritage-listed Mungo National Park is very different. Once covered in lakes, the region dried up at the end of the last ice age. History was made here in 1968 when a geologist stumbled upon the 26 000-year-old cremated remains of a woman – proof, along with other remains, of the world's earliest known cultural and spiritual practices.

North across the border in outback Queensland, the towns add another dimension to past and present experience of the Australian outback. Connected by a network of lonely highways and developmental roads built by mining companies, these towns are hundreds of kilometres apart.

Once a camp ground for shearers, the outback Queensland town of Longreach has gained fame as the birthplace of Qantas – the national air carrier that made its inaugural flight from there in 1922. In more recent times, Longreach attracts visitors to its Australian Stockman's Hall of Fame, honouring the pioneering stockmen and women who opened up the outback.

PREVIOUS PAGES In the golden afternoon light, a wind sock fills beside the dirt airstrip of Carisbrooke Station, near Winton.

OPPOSITE Looking out from Mount Poole, named by Charles Sturt after Poole's death from scurvy.

19

Mootwingee National Park

RIGHT A wide almost dry creek bed, en route to Mootwingee
National Park from Broken Hill, provides a picturesque insight into
the seasonal nature of the Australian outback.

BELOW A cave wall covered in ancient hand stencils pays testimony
to the Aboriginal people who once lived in the traditional lands now
known as Mootwingee National Park.

FOLLOWING PAGES Moody storm light casts a pinkish glow across a
string of eroded sand dunes. Found in the ancient domain of Mungo
National Park, the dunes are known as the Walls of China.

20

OPPOSITE TOP Long-dead eucalypts form an eerie network of bare branches at dusk on the Cawndilla–Menindee Lake System in Kinchega National Park in remote south-western New South Wales.

BOTTOM RIGHT This enormous old woolshed, complete with corrugated iron roof, survives from the time when Kinchega was a thriving sheep station.

BOTTOM LEFT The shearers of Australia's outback are the country's unsung heroes. Here Andrew Mawson sets to work in the original shearing shed of Isis Downs Station.

BELOW The Darling River cuts through the seemingly unending treeless green plains of the far-flung Kinchega National Park, eroding the earth to reveal a curious pattern of ochre striations.

EARLY EXPLORERS

Driven by the need for new grazing pastures, three landholders – Blaxland, Lawson and Wentworth – crossed the Blue Mountains in 1813. Their success dropped the flag on an era of some 50 years which saw the massive push west to open the entire continent to European settlers.

Charles Sturt was one of the greatest explorers. His 1844 expedition dispelled the then popular belief in an inland sea, reporting that land at the continent's heart was little more than saltpans and stony deserts. A memorial to an expedition member, James Poole, stands at Depot Glen (see above). His contemporary, Ludwig Leichhardt, immortalised as Voss in Patrick White's novel of the same name, was not so successful in his attempt to cross northern Australia from east to west. Leichhardt and his party disappeared without a trace. His death remains a mystery, though it's believed he had a confrontation with Aborigines near the junction of the Georgina and Diamantina rivers.

Burke and Wills are another two famous explorers. Renowned for their expedition to establish a north–south link, they succeeded in reaching the Gulf of Carpentaria only to die near Innamincka on the return journey.

OPPOSITE Australia earned its wealth earlier this century 'riding on the sheep's back'. In a typical outback scene, sheep are loaded from the saleyards of Swan Hill.

ABOVE Founded on great mineral wealth, Broken Hill retains many glorious turn-of-the-century buildings, including the Palace Hotel with its ornate wrought-iron lace balconies.

BELOW Established in the early 1860s as a centre for the surrounding sheep stations, Bourke remains one of the world's major centres for the transshipment of wool.

LEFT The Qantas Founders Outback Museum is housed in the original hangar used by Qantas, Australia's national airline. The airline was founded in nearby Charleville in 1921. The following year, Longreach became its operational base and Australia's first seven aircraft were built here between 1922 and 1930.

BELOW A statue outside Longreach's Stockman's Hall of Fame celebrates the stockmen and women who played a vital role in opening up Australia's outback, riding out from Longreach to drove cattle along some of the country's most infamous and hazardous stock routes.

OPPOSITE Cattle are scattered across a vast empty plain beside the road near Carisbrooke Station, out of Winton. Hardy strains of cattle have been bred to survive in the harsh semi-arid country which sprawls west toward the desert areas of central Australia.

RIGHT The Waltzing Matilda Centenary Billabong commemorates the fact that 'Waltzing Matilda', Australia's unofficial national anthem, was first performed in Winton. Banjo Paterson penned it after visiting a nearby waterhole where a shearer had once committed suicide.

BELOW The post box at Carisbrooke Station. For outback residents, mail delivery is generally a once-a-week occurrence and communication with the outside world is more often by telephone.

THE SOUTH

THE SOUTH
From Oodnadatta to the Nullarbor

The Australian outback is epitomised by the majestic Flinders Ranges of South Australia. Much painted and photographed for their grand beauty, the ranges begin just 200 kilometres north of the state capital, Adelaide.

These ancient mountains, thrust up from the sea some 1.6 billion years ago, are the traditional home of the Adnyamathanha, or 'hill people'. Thought to have inhabited the area for some 12 000 years, they have left much evidence of their long history in the region – art sites abound, mostly of rock engravings or petroglyphs.

The first European to see the ranges was Matthew Flinders. He sighted the mountains from the deck of his ship as it sailed up the large body of water now called Spencer Gulf, and sent out a party to climb one of its highest peaks – Mount Remarkable.

Forty years were to pass before Edward John Eyre began to explore the inhospitable western reaches of the Flinders dotted with salt lakes, the largest of which was named in his honour. By 1851, pastoralists had arrived and the Wilpena, Aroona and Arkaba runs had been established. Two of these sprawling stations now make up the Flinders Ranges National Park.

The Flinders Ranges are spectacular with their bent and buckled formations. Rising to form an abrupt escarpment, they are known for their mysteriously changing colours which range from gentle desert pinks and mauves to vibrant reds and yellows. Criss-crossed by fabulous, although often challenging, walking tracks, the ranges are softened in spring by a carpet of wildflowers, including the handsome red and black Sturt's desert pea – South Australia's state flower.

Wilpena Pound in the southern ranges is one of the most sensational geological features of the Flinders. It is also the most dramatic visual feature, forming a natural amphitheatre 11 kilometres long and 5 kilometres wide. A range slopes gently up from the inside to end in a sheer line of bluffs dropping sharply to encircle the Pound. On the north-western extremity is St Mary Peak – the highest point in South Australia.

Amidst the rugged mountains, gorges and quartzite plateau formations of the northern Flinders lies the Gammon Ranges National Park. The famous RM Williams stockmen's equipment business began here at a bush camp at Italowie Gap – now a popular bushwalking and picnicking destination.

West of the Finders Ranges many salt lakes stretch across the top of the Eyre Peninsula. Further west the Nullarbor Plain drops sharply into the Southern Ocean. *Null arbor* is Latin for 'no trees' and though this is not literally the case, it communicates the vast and flat emptiness of this great limestone plateau. Crossing the Nullarbor is considered by many to be the ultimate drive – 1200 kilometres from Ceduna in the east to Norseman in Western Australia. The scenery is desolate and dramatic, particularly the last section before the border which is now proclaimed as the Nullarbor National Park. Here the road passes along sheer cliffs with spectacular views of the Great Australian Bight.

North towards Alice Springs, spectacular sandstone outcrops known as the Breakaways can be seen in low hills of the Stuart Ranges near the opal town of Coober Pedy – home to some of the outback's more eccentric characters. Here opal prospectors live underground to escape the relentless heat which reaches up to 50°C in summer.

For those seeking a more serious adventure, the Strzelecki Track starts from the town of Lyndhurst on the northern edge of the Flinders Ranges and runs 560 kilometres north to Innamincka on Cooper Creek.

PREVIOUS PAGES A young girl waits at a petrol pump in the middle of nowhere, at ease with the big open spaces.
OPPOSITE A stretch of road across the Nullarbor Plain runs ruler-straight for over 100 kilometres.

RIGHT At 1190 metres St Mary Peak, on the edge of Wilpena Pound in the Flinders Ranges, is the highest mountain in South Australia.

OPPOSITE TOP Forming an unexpectedly eerie landscape, the Breakaways are a vibrantly colourful low range of sandstone outcrops that form a separate and distinct part of the Stuart Ranges near Coober Pedy.

BELOW With the bluffs of the Heysen Range looming on the horizon, this pretty stretch of country is in the heart of the Flinders Ranges National Park.

ABOVE Typically after rain, the Sturt's desert pea will flower, forming a carpet of brilliant red flowers over the sandy roadside terrain.

LEFT The emu is a large, flightless bird endemic to Australia; it has roamed the continent for two million years.

OPPOSITE TOP Seen from the Oodnadatta Track, Lake Eyre covers 9700 square kilometres and is Australia's largest salt lake. The lake is rarely filled but during flood it is a breeding ground for waterbirds.

BELOW The rugged Gammon Ranges, renowned today for their challenging walking tracks, were first crossed by Europeans in 1847.

ABOVE The famed Pink Roadhouse at Oodnadatta (an Aboriginal word meaning 'the yellow flower of the mulga tree') provides outback travellers with supplies and respite from the surrounding hundreds of miles of outback.

RIGHT A road train transports stock from station to market. An everyday sight for drivers on outback roads, these giant transport vehicles travel at high speeds. It's etiquette, and safer, to give way to them.

OPPOSITE BOTTOM This sign, with its unusual trio of hazards, is a typical feature of the long, endless roads that stretch across the Nullarbor Plain.

OPALS

Australia produces approximately 95 per cent of the world's precious opal. Most of it comes from the town of Coober Pedy, the largest and oldest opal mining centre in the country. Coober Pedy is an Aboriginal name meaning 'white fellow's hole in the ground', and was given because in this unusual outback town most residents live underground to escape the above-ground heat. Many 'dugouts' are as large as regular houses and, other than an absence of windows, look like normal houses inside.

Opal was discovered in Coober Pedy in 1915 and, today, surrounded by a moon-like landscape with a surface pitted by nearly a century of diggings, Coober Pedy now has a population of some 3500, many originally from far-flung corners of the globe. Visitors to opal mining towns such as Coober Pedy can go on mine tours and see opals cut and polished.

Australian opals were formed during the Tertiary Period. In the Cretaceous Period (65 to 140 million years ago), what is now arid central Australia was an inland sea. In the subsequent Tertiary Period, ground water rich in silica permeated sedimentary rocks through openings caused by faults and dissolved matter. The solidification of these areas created opal.

ABOVE Henrik Schreber is a self-confessed eccentric of Coober Pedy, a town where the majority of the population live in underground dugouts because of temperature extremes.

OPPOSITE The outback is full of unexpected and unusual landforms and South Australia's Painted Desert, is a perfect example. Located on the route between Coober Pedy and Oodnadatta, it is a pastel-coloured collection of mesa hills scattered across a plain.

BELOW Making the most of his underground home, which featured in the movie *Mad Max*, Crocodile Harry has decorated his windowless walls with outlandish sculptures and graffiti.

RIGHT Not far from Ceduna is the equally remote town of Penong, a settlement famed for its forest of windmills which capture the cool ocean breezes from the Great Australian Bight.

BELOW The scenery of the Great Australian Bight is magnificent and unique. The vast flatness of the Nullarbor Plain runs straight to the cliffs, which drop dramatically into the ocean, almost as if they were sheered off in millennia past in one swift motion.

THE CORNER
COUNTRY

THE CORNER COUNTRY

Where the States Meet

To the west of Bourke and the north of Broken Hill lies the Corner Country, so-called because it centres around the meeting of the New South Wales, Queensland and South Australian borders. Reached by the Silver City Highway, the Corner Country is extremely tough terrain and supports only one sheep for every eight hectares.

Towns in this part of the world are as outback as they come. Tibooburra, meaning 'place of granite', is the most remote town in New South Wales. It is also the hottest town in the state with summer temperatures reaching as high as 50°C. Born of a goldrush in the late 1800s, Tibooburra now supports the pastoral industry of outlying stations. With a population of less than 100, it is a 'two pub' town – the Family Hotel is renowned for its shady verandah and stands directly across the road from the Tibooburra Hotel.

People who venture this far off the beaten track are usually heading for the Sturt National Park – a vast tract of red sandhills, mulga scrub and mesas in the far north-west corner of the state. Like many modern-day national parks, the Sturt National Park is a conglomeration of old stations. Originally six sheep stations, the park runs for 80 kilometres along the Queensland border from Cameron Corner – the point where the three states meet, surveyed by John Cameron in 1880.

The Sturt National Park is dominated by the spectacular Grey Range – giant bluffs of sandstone that rise 150 metres above rust-red plains. As well as its unique and dramatic scenery, Sturt National Park has an abundance of wildlife; typically western grey and red kangaroos, emus, wedge-tailed eagles and kestrels are easy to spot within its bounds.

North across the border is another type of terrain again. Known as the Channel Country, the south-western corner of Queensland derives its name from the complex network of watercourses in the region. This area is either very wet or very dry. When it does rain, the whole area floods into a massive lake system. It is a stunning sight from the air, but on the ground stations can remain cut off for months.

The Diamantina Developmental Road provides the main route through the Channel Country, as well as access to the north end of the Birdsville Track.

Birdsville is Queensland's most remote town, famous for its pub and for the Birdsville Races which annually swell the town's population of 100 to over 5000, many punters arriving by light plane. Birdsville started out as a store on the Diamantina River in 1872 when it was the last stop for stockmen driving cattle south to the markets at Adelaide.

From Birdsville, it's a short drive to the Simpson Desert National Park and Poeppel Corner, where the borders of South Australia, the Northern Territory and Queensland meet. The exact point is indicated by a replica of the original coolabah marker. The national park takes up only one million hectares of the waterless 20-million-hectare Simpson Desert.

Extending south from the south-western corner of Queensland into South Australia and north as far as the Northern Territory's MacDonnell Ranges, the Simpson is the largest sand-dune desert in the world. The remnants of a huge mountain range that once straddled Australia, its sand dunes are stable and run north–south in the direction of the prevailing winds. Though one of the harshest terrains on earth, the Simpson receives around 100 millimetres of rain per year and has a curious diversity of life, from snakes and lizards to tiny hopping mice, the rare marsupial mole, and desert birds such as the colourful spinifex parrot.

PREVIOUS PAGES At 5490 kilometres, the world's longest artificial barrier, the Dog Fence, keeps dingoes from sheep flocks in the continent's south-east.

OPPOSITE Poeppel Corner in the Simpson Desert marks the meeting point of the Northern Territory, Queensland and South Australia.

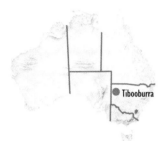

Tibooburra

RIGHT Founded in 1881 when gold was discovered 40 kilometres to the north, Tibooburra survives as a classic Australian outback town. This shot of Tibooburra's main, and only, street illustrates the typically wide open thoroughfares and relaxed atmosphere that exists in the towns of the interior. Here it is so hot, one is forced to move slowly or not at all. Today Tibooburra services residents of one of the country's most isolated sheep farming districts. It also provides travellers with a friendly last supply post before they head out to explore Sturt National Park and Cameron Corner.

ABOVE Perched on a vast rock-strewn plain, Cordillo Downs is typical of the homesteads which provide the hardy graziers of the semi-arid Corner Country with some respite from the harsh conditions.

LEFT Stunning red sand dunes such as this one receive an extremely unreliable average annual rainfall, yet manage to support a surprisingly wide variety of tenacious plant and animal life.

BELOW Cameron Corner, 140 kilometres west of Tibooburra, is the official meeting point of three states – Queensland, New South Wales and South Australia. Named after the government surveyor, John Cameron, who originally surveyed the border, it's an historic site on the Strzelecki Track – a stock route pioneered in 1870 when Harry Redford stole a herd of cattle and drove them south to Adelaide.

OPPOSITE TOP Horses race across a wide open dirt plain in the renowned Birdsville Races, a two-day race meeting held every September in the outback town of Birdsville.

RIGHT AND BELOW Country race meetings are increasingly popular events in Australia, and the Birdsville Races are probably the most famous. They are known for attracting a great number of guests, some of whom arrive by light aircraft. Plane travel is quite common in the outback and, given the huge distances, it is a sensible way of getting around.

DESERT FLORA

After rain, the Australian desert is transformed into a carpet of brilliant wildflowers. They are mostly short-lived plants such as daisies, pussy tails and pea flowers, but while they last they are amazingly brilliant and pro-fuse, a joy to see. The miracle of the desert flowering is due to the seeds of the plants – these can lie dormant for years until the right mix of tempera-ture and moisture occurs. The flower-ing brings with it a burst of activity from nectar-drinking birds and insects. But even during the Dry, the Aust-ralian desert is surprising. Look down to the arid earth that surrounds the great rock of Uluru and you will see tiny delicate blooms growing boldly out of the red sand.

There are many other plants and trees which have adapted to the harsh interior. About 60 species of eucalypt grow in the desert, notably the river red gum, found in the beautiful gorges of the centre, and the ghost gum with its bright green leaves and glossy white bark. Wattle, Australia's floral emblem, is another prolific flowering tree of the interior. Mulga, with its leaves which are resistant to water loss, is wide-spread too, as is saltbush, the only plant to be seen for kilometres on the Oodnadatta and Birdsville tracks.

RIGHT Seen from the air, the pale sands of the Diamantina flood plains and the red Simpson Desert dunes outside Birdsville appear lifeless. In fact, fed by the Diamantina River, this country is dotted with coolabah trees and hardy lignum bushes and is home to majestic dancing brolgas.

BELOW The rich red dunes of the Simpson Desert reach up to 20 metres in height and can run for kilometres in a series of unbroken parallel lines. Signs warn travellers of the danger of oncoming traffic.

RIGHT Seen at dawn, the Dalhousie Springs in the Witjira National Park appear swathed in a gentle mist. Providing a delightful respite from the surrounding arid terrain, the springs are a significant source of food and water for the Aboriginal inhabitants of the area.

BELOW The crumbling chimneystacks of the old Dalhousie homestead in the Witjira National Park, located to the west of Poeppel Corner, pay testimony to the early pioneering days of the late 1890s.

THE NORTH

THE NORTH
The Gulf Country and Tropical Outback

The upper reaches of the Northern Territory and far north Queensland are wild tropical domains ruled, for the most part, by a monsoonal climate. Ranging from the sprawling wetlands and lily pad-covered billabongs of Kakadu, through the towering red cliffs of the Katherine Gorge and the Arnhem Land escarpment to the remote savannahs of Cape York, it is a world of lush and colourful landscapes and raw majestic beauty.

With high humidity and a year-round average temperature in the low thirties, the Top End – the northern tropical and semi-tropical region of the Northern Territory – is a balmy world in which the eternal recurring of the Wet, the rainy season, and the Dry gives birth to a rich and complex cycle of life.

The Stuart Highway, called simply 'the track' by locals, runs south-east from Darwin, the capital of the Northern Territory, through tropical woodland to the next major town of Katherine. Along the way the Arnhem Highway branches off to Kakadu National Park.

Kakadu is just a 250-kilometre drive from Darwin. In the context of the Australian outback, where distances are so vast that much of the population receives their mail by plane, this is a comparatively short distance.

Granted World Heritage status for its exceptional natural and cultural attributes, Kakadu is a world unto itself. It covers some 20 000 square kilometres and encompasses the entire South Alligator River System.

Kakadu incorporates all the major habitat types of the Top End. Some of its most famous sites are the bird sanctuary wetlands of Yellow Waters; Nourlangie and Ubirr rocks with their brilliant ancient rock paintings dating back tens of thousands of years; and the dramatic escarpment waterfalls, Twin and Jim Jim Falls. Traditional land of the Gagadju people, Kakadu is thought to have been inhabited by Aboriginal people for at least 50 000 years. Arnhem Land, which takes up the eastern half of the Top End, is entirely Aboriginal land. A few specialist tour operators take travellers into Arnhem Land, but permits and special permission from traditional land owners are required.

From Roper Bar on the edge of Arnhem Land, travellers with a yen for adventure can drive the Gulf Track over to Cape York. Traversing some of the wildest terrain in tropical Australia, this track follows in the footsteps of explorer Ludwig Leichhardt and legendary stockmen such as Nat 'Bluey' Buchanan, who first drove 1200 cattle across to Darwin in 1878. The track, which became the main stock route from the Top End to Queensland, is dotted with graves and is rich in amazing tales of courage. It is possible to take detours to the Gulf of Carpentaria for stunning coastal scenery and fishing.

A part of the outback that has its own unique atmosphere is Cape York. The size of Victoria but with a population of only around 1500, the Cape is one of the last frontiers. For a vivid sense of the region's history, many travellers set out from Cooktown where Captain Cook oversaw repairs to the *Endeavour* in 1770. From this last outpost, the Cape becomes an increasingly wild world of vast, little-visited national parks, sprawling cattle stations and Aboriginal lands such as the escarpment country around Laura. This is home to the Quinkan rock paintings – some of the world's most significant prehistoric art.

To the south lie the outback mining towns of Mount Isa and Cloncurry, where John Flynn began the Royal Flying Doctor Service in 1927. If it weren't for these towns, this parched region of the outback would have very little human presence.

PREVIOUS PAGES Cattle provide the livelihood for many outback people and are often driven long distances in search of water.

OPPOSITE Gum trees, ochre-coloured earth and a cloudless sky – scenery typical of the Top End.

Kakadu National Park

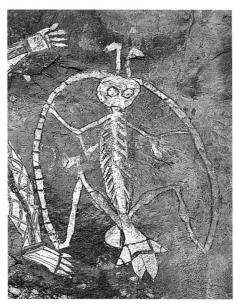

ABOVE The dramatic sandstone cliffs of Kakadu shelter some 5000 Aboriginal rock art sites. Painted in yellow, red and white they depict the material and spiritual life of the Aboriginal people of Kakadu. Images include animals, mythical figures and even European ships.

LEFT The jabiru, or black-necked stork, is an elegant bird that feeds on small crustaceans and fish. It is a common sight in the wetlands of Australia's northern reaches and, along with numerous other species of waterbird, can be seen at Kakadu National Park's Yellow Water – a giant wetland which is also home to the intimidating saltwater crocodile.

OPPOSITE Several waterfalls tumble down the 600-kilometre-long escarpment that runs through Kakadu National Park. Most of them are seasonal – thundering torrents during the Wet, but generally reduced to mere trickles during the Dry.

CAMELS

Camels and their Afghan cameleers played a key role in settling the outback. The first camels were imported to Adelaide in the 1840s by John Horrocks who used them on his expedition into the area north of Spencer Gulf. Soon after, Burke and Wills used camels for their ill-fated expedition.

With their ability to carry hefty loads and survive for long periods without water, camels were ideally suited to the harsh dry conditions that prevailed in most of the outback. In the laying of the Overland Telegraph Line from Adelaide to Darwin, camels were used to transport the telegraph poles and to haul rock to repeater stations. Most famously, they worked from the railhead in South Australia's Oodnadatta delivering mail and supplies to remote stations and settlements.

Known as 'ships of the desert', in their heyday around 12 000 camels were operating in the outback. They carried up to 600 kilograms each, working camel 'pads' or tracks which criss-crossed the outback. When the railway to Alice Springs was eventually completed, the train was named The Ghan in honour of the Afghan cameleers. Today, of the 18 introduced mammal species now feral in the Australian outback, the camel is the largest in number.

Arnhem Land
Katherine Gorge

OPPOSITE TOP Aboriginal customs are still upheld in Arnhem Land, with dancers gathering to perform at traditional corroborees.

RIGHT With its spectacular flood plains, gorges and escarpments, Arnhem Land is one of the few areas on the Australian continent that has remained largely unaffected by white settlement.

BELOW Together with Kakadu, Katherine Gorge is one of the main attractions of the Top End. Eroded over millennia by the permanently flowing Katherine River, the gorge is actually made up of 13 canyons. Cut through the sandstone of the Arnhem Plateau, it is best seen during the Dry and is most popularly viewed by boat.

ABOVE Working in the outback of the Top End is an extremely hot and dusty business. Here a stockman near Kakadu smiles despite the heat.

LEFT These massive termite mounds are a striking and enigmatic feature of the Litchfield landscape. In order to minimise exposure to the midday sun, they are aligned in a north–south direction – a feature which has led to them being described as 'magnetic'.

BELOW The Daly Waters pub is reputed to be the oldest hotel in the Northern Territory. It is also the heartbeat of the tiny community of Daly Waters. Draped in bougainvillea and featuring traditional outback architecture to maximise shade and catch the breezes, it is a must on a hot journey through the northern reaches.

ABOVE It is hard to believe that at the end of this seemingly endless road lie the tropical waters of the Gulf of Carpentaria. Until this road linking Normanton to the coastal town of Karumba was built, the only access to this stretch of coast was by boat.

OPPOSITE TOP In its heyday, Croydon was a thriving town whose fortune was based on mining. The Club Hotel was established in 1887, two years after the discovery of gold.

OPPOSITE BOTTOM Karumba, located on the Gulf of Carpentaria at the mouth of the Norman River, is an important fishing port of the Top End. Its wetlands and estuaries extend inland for several kilometres and are home to the much sought-after barramundi.

Cape York

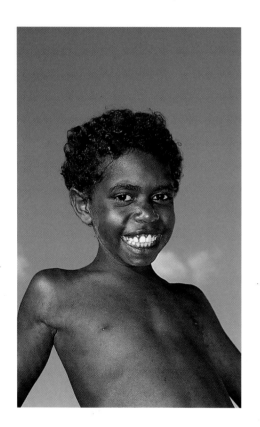

ABOVE A smiling Torres Strait Islander boy
from the idyllic and remote town of Seisia
on Cape York in far north Queensland.

RIGHT The vast Cape York Peninsula is rugged
and largely uninhabited. The coastal township
of Somerset was established in 1863 and was
Australia's most northerly settlement. Today,
however, it is abandoned and the coast lies
undisturbed once more.

OPPOSITE TOP The main street of Cooktown is lined by grand late-19th century buildings that were constructed during the town's heyday as a port for the Palmer River goldfields.

OPPOSITE BOTTOM Fishermen line the bridge over the Annan River outside Cooktown. Most northern rivers deserve a healthy respect because of the presence of saltwater crocodiles.

BELOW The Jardine River National Park is situated near the northern tip of Cape York and covers over 230 000 hectares, including most of the Jardine River's catchment area. Rainforest, eucalypts, heaths and swamps combine to create an area of great scenic diversity.

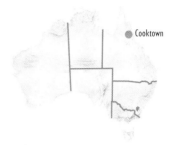

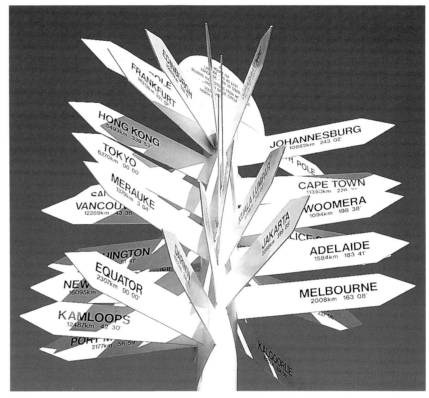

ABOVE Surrounded by hundreds of kilometres of arid plains, the town of Mount Isa services a network of isolated cattle stations. Experiencing a hot dry climate, it is also a town with significant mineral wealth and the gateway to Lawn Hill National Park, as well as Riversleigh – a region which harbours a wealth of prehistoric fossils.

TOP RIGHT 'Far from everywhere' seems to be the message of this sign located at Mount Isa's lookout!

RIGHT The Royal Flying Doctor Service was founded by the Rev. John Flynn in 1927 in the outback Queensland town of Cloncurry. In the Flynn Museum, a reconstructed office shows how staff operated in the early years, establishing Flynn's vision of a 'mantle of safety' over the people of the outback.

OPPOSITE BOTTOM A 'tent house' in the suburbs of Mount Isa shows how different materials and designs are adapted to construct homes suited to the relentless local climate.

THE CENTRE

THE CENTRE
Australia's Heartland

Australia's red centre is a mesmerising land of vast scrub-covered desert plains crossed by ancient gnarled mountain ranges which are cut through with spectacular gorges and waterholes. The geographical and spiritual heart of this country is the majestic rock Uluru and the nearby multi-domed Katatjuta.

The largest monolith on earth, Uluru has long been of great significance to the Anangu, its traditional custodians. Today the rock is a national icon, the goal of modern-day pilgrims who come from all over the world to see its different moods. Elusive and ever-changing, Uluru is most often photographed at sunset when it glows the colour of hot coals. It is equally captivating at other times of the day when it ranges from dusky mauve to purple brown and a strident rust red. Uluru exudes a mystery enhanced by the Dreamtime stories of its traditional owners, who tell how the great rock and nearby Katatjuta came into being.

Much of the area is known for its ochre colour and is thus often referred to as the 'red centre'. The arid heart of the driest continent on earth after Antarctica, it is a timeless and harsh landscape with a rare and peaceful majesty. It is a place of unexpected beauty, of sage-green plains, fine white-trunked ghost gums growing on red ridgelines backed by a cloudless blue sky and deep blue-black night skies studded with stars.

The essence of this desert country is captured in the dot and circle paintings of Western Desert Aborigines. The sand drawings which were once created as part of ceremonies have now been transposed into the modern art form of painting. For many who travel to Australia's centre, these gentle depictions of the desert recall an aerial perspective of the desert's curious striations, landforms and clusters of vegetation.

Though the desert lands of the centre may initially appear as lifeless as a lunar landscape, this is not the case. In any part of the centre, the sandy soil reveals a world of tiny footprints. Many larger native animals are also to be found including the handsome red kangaroo, the euro or hill kangaroo, the black-footed rock-wallaby and the emu, to name but a few. One thing all the creatures of the outback have in common – they are tenacious survivors, well adapted to the rigorous conditions needed to live in one of the harshest environments on earth.

The main human settlement in the centre, and the most popular jumping-off point for travellers visiting Uluru and the sites of the region, is the town of Alice Springs. The Alice, as it is known by locals, was founded in 1871 as one of Australia's first telegraph stations, establishing a key link in the overland telegraph from Adelaide to Darwin. The telegraph station played a crucial role in the development of the outback, reducing the isolation of early settlers.

Strung out along the gum-lined Todd River bed and bounded by the imposingly craggy MacDonnell Ranges which run to the east and west, cutting a reptile-like swath across the surrounding plains for some 500 kilometres, Alice Springs is definitely something of an oasis in the outback.

Remnants of a mountain range that would have stood as high as the Himalayas, the ragged MacDonnell Ranges have been worn down by thousands of years of sun, wind and rain. This rust-red range – formed from a hard rock termed by geologists as Heavitree quartzite – is the catchment area of the centre, protecting a string of spectacular gorges which secure and preserve scarce rainwater and sustain sheltered waterholes that remain well filled even in the Dry.

PREVIOUS PAGES 'Discovered' by John McDouall Stuart in 1860, this outcrop of red sandstone in the Simpson Desert is known as Chambers Pillar.
OPPOSITE Paddymelon vines flourish like weeds in the disturbed soil beside the Plenty Highway.

Uluru–Katatjuta N.P.

OPPOSITE A group of people walking in the Olgas Gorge in Katatjuta (formerly the Olgas). There are two walks that meander through the formation's 36 domes, introducing visitors to an eerie and beautiful world.

BELOW The great rock at the heart of this continent glows luminously in the fading afternoon light. Seen here from the air, Uluru appears like some giant ancient beast crouched on the plains. Measuring 9.4 kilometres around its base and rising 348 metres, the rock is both immense and imposing. To the Anangu, the traditional inhabitants of the area, Uluru has great spiritual significance and, though it is still a popular pastime, climbing the rock is not approved of by them.

ABORIGINAL ART

With the returning of traditional Aboriginal lands there has been a resurgence of indigenous culture. In the central desert country, sand drawings created during ceremonies are reinvented in modern circle and dot painting style. Such paintings are sold not only in Alice Springs, but also in the auction rooms of Paris and New York.

Another way in which Aboriginal culture is being revived and shared with non-Aboriginal people is through indigenous tourism – Aboriginal people taking visitors into their traditional lands. Uluru and Katatjuta were returned to their traditional owners in October 1985. On the 10th anniversary, a cultural interpretative centre was opened. It is a place where indigenous art and crafts are displayed and the cultural significance of the area to the Anangu people is explained. Anangu Tours, an Aboriginal-owned company, takes visitors on walks, introducing local bush medicine and tucker. Another group, the tourism award-winning Manyallaluk, takes people on tours out of Katherine, setting up bush camps and walking out to remote art sites and pristine waterholes.

LEFT Late afternoon sun lights up the cliffs of Kings Canyon, giving them a rich golden hue. The enormous proportions of the canyon are brought into perspective by the ant-like human figures silhouetted on the ridge line. A massive cleft in the George Gill Range, Kings Canyon is topped by a myriad of dome-shaped 'beehives' known as the Lost City, as well as a stunning rockpool known as the Garden of Eden.

BELOW Finke Gorge National Park is the only place in the world where red cabbage palms have been found to grow naturally. The species has existed here for at least 10 000 years and these particular palms, located in the appropriately named Palm Valley, have taken several hundred years to grow to their present height.

FOLLOWING PAGES Forming part of the MacDonnell Ranges, Finke Gorge's terracotta-coloured cliffs have been gradually eroded over millennia. They are still a striking sight, however, in an otherwise predominantly flat landscape.

ABOVE A view from Anzac Hill of Alice Springs backed by the MacDonnell Ranges. Considered the capital of the centre, Alice Springs gained world-wide recognition as the setting for Neville Shute's novel *A Town Like Alice*, which was later made into a film of the same name.

LEFT Hot-air ballooning is a popular pursuit in the outback town of Alice Springs and provides a unique way for travellers to see the surrounding landscape. Rising early, ballooners prepare their balloons before dawn, setting out just as the sun creeps over the horizon.

OPPOSITE The Henley-on-Todd Regatta is held annually in the dry bed of the Todd River, which runs through Alice Springs. The 'boats' competing in the regatta are powered by foot.

ABOVE With rainbow-like bands of colour appearing in the brilliant early morning and late afternoon light, this dramatic sandstone outcrop is located in the aptly named Rainbow Valley. Part of the James Range south of Alice Springs, it is surrounded by spinifex-covered sand plains and a network of interconnecting claypans.

LEFT This young dingo at Ellery Creek in the MacDonnell Ranges is surprisingly friendly. Thought to have migrated with early Aborigines tens of thousands of years ago, dingoes are now so common in the Australian outback they are considered a native animal.

OPPOSITE The yellow-footed rock-wallaby has excellent camouflage and is common to the rocky outcrops and gorges of south-central Australia.

92

OPPOSITE This enticing waterhole in Glen Helen Gorge has been carved out of the surrounding rock by the Finke River, which drains into the Simpson Desert to the south.

BELOW The Devils Marbles are mysterious granite boulders scattered across a plain to the south of Tennant Creek. The Warumungu people consider the rocks to be the eggs of the mythical Rainbow Serpent.

FOLLOWING PAGES This overview of the town of Tennant Creek, from a neighbouring hill, highlights the starkly arid but brilliant red-ochre coloured earth that typifies the central desert regions.

THE WEST

THE WEST

From the Desert to the Sea

Taking up the far north-western corner of Western Australia is a rugged 350 000-square-kilometre region known as the Kimberley. Bigger than the United Kingdom, it is bounded to the north and west by a ragged twisted coastline, and to the south and east by a line of craggy sandstone ranges. The Kimberley is reached via the rough and unpredictable Gibb River Road which was once used to transport cattle from the Kimberley to the ports of Derby and Wyndham. Today the Kimberley is still home to huge cattle stations as well as isolated Aboriginal communities and national parks.

For hundreds of years, Macassarese bêche-de-mer fishermen from the islands of Indonesia sailed to the Kimberley coast. The local Aborigines next came into contact with outsiders when European pastoralists tried to find grazing land, only to be frustrated until they discovered the Fitzroy and Ord rivers in the late-19th century. Pastoralist families such as the Buchanans and the Durack family settled in the area, while a booming pearling industry began in the coastal town of Broome.

Today, the Kimberley remains a vast and wild expanse. A world of adventure is contained in this region, but highlights include Windjana Gorge with its 90-metre-high multicoloured cliffs; Geikie Gorge, which is best viewed by boat; and Tunnel Creek, where water has worn its way beneath the range creating a 750-metre tunnel now populated by bats. A hundred years ago, the caves were the hideout of the Aboriginal bushranger Jandamarra and his gang.

Some distance to the south-east is a region that is probably the Kimberley's most famous. The Bungle Bungles (Purnululu) is an area of enormous sandstone domes with magnificent horizontal bands produced by rust-red siliceous sandstone and darker layers coloured by black lichens. Most spectacular when viewed from the air, the Bungle Bungles only became known to the general public in 1983. Though access is difficult, which is probably just as well since the domes are very fragile and sensitive to erosion, the Bungle Bungles have become an increasingly popular Kimberley destination.

Travellers to the Bungle Bungles often use the north-eastern town of Kununurra as their base. Founded in the 1960s, Kununurra is at the heart of the Ord River Irrigation Scheme, a venture that tempers the climatic extremes of the Wet and the Dry and has encouraged agriculture on a grand scale. Lake Argyle, the main water reservoir, contains nine times as much water as Sydney Harbour and is a delightful oasis in a predominantly arid domain.

Kununurra is also the main service centre for the Argyle Diamond Mine which lies some 250 kilometres to the south. One of the world's largest diamond mines, the Argyle produces about 35 per cent of world diamond supplies.

The Pilbara, lying south of the Kimberley and encompassing over 500 000 square kilometres of isolated terrain, is exceptionally rich in minerals and has the world's greatest surface deposits of iron ore. One of the most ancient places on earth, the Pilbara stretches inland from the coast to the edges of the Great Sandy and Gibson deserts. The remote Karijini National Park lies deep in the heart of the Pilbara, home to a string of breathtakingly beautiful gorges carved from the rugged Hamersley Ranges.

Further to the south lies another great mining town of outback Western Australia – Kalgoorlie. Retaining the air of a frontier town, it reached its peak as a gold town around the turn of the century. Elegant streets of gracious residences and shops remain in testimony to the town's glory days.

PREVIOUS PAGES Early morning light warms the wheat-coloured sands and limestone pillars covering the Pinnacles Desert in Nambung National Park.

OPPOSITE The Zuytdorp Cliffs, pounded by the might of the Indian Ocean, are named after a Dutch vessel wrecked there in 1712.

ABOVE Cut through the rugged Napier Range by the Lennard River, the spectacular Windjana Gorge is a long narrow canyon with near-vertical walls for almost all its length. Cool freshwater pools offer respite for visitors and local wildlife such as freshwater crocodiles and rock walla-bies. Made up of reef structures with exposed layers of fossils, the gorge was once home to the extinct diprotodon, a giant marsupial said to look like a cross between a rhino and a wombat.

RIGHT Carved out by the Fitzroy River, Geikie Gorge exposes a window onto the past – a section of Devonian reef consisting of limestone embedded with layers of fossils.

100

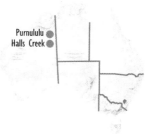

LEFT The Prison Tree is an enormous hollow boab tree which was used in pioneering days as an overnight lockup. Measuring 14 metres around its widest point, the tree is said to be 1500 years old.

BELOW The remnants of a mud brick post office in Old Halls Creek recall the time when the town was the site of Western Australia's first gold rush. Nowadays, the nearby 'new town', is the hub of the region's beef industry and gateway to the gruelling four-wheel-drive Canning Stock Route.

FOLLOWING PAGES The beehive formations of the Bungle Bungles (Purnululu) are an extraordinary sight. Soft ochre-coloured sandstone eroded by wind and sun, they are at their most spectacular when seen from the air.

ABOVE The sprawling Lake Argyle, Australia's largest artificial lake, was created as part of the Ord River Irrigation Scheme – a massive irrigation project.

LEFT Moderating the extremes of the Wet and the Dry, irrigation brings a workable year-round water supply to the Kununurra region, allowing local landowners to grow and harvest a diverse range of crops such as watermelon for export to southern markets.

OPPOSITE BOTTOM Located in the Carr–Boyd Range, the Argyle Diamond Mine is one of the world's largest diamond mines, producing 17 kilograms of diamonds a day.

DIAMOND MINING

World famous for its 'cognac' or 'champagne' diamonds, the huge open-cut Argyle Diamond Mine is located some 200 kilometres south of Kununurra in Western Australia. Officially known as AK1, Argyle Kiberlite One, the site took seven years of intensive exploration by scientific teams to find.

Interest had initially been sparked between the two world wars, when a man named Watson came in to Kalumburu Mission in the far north-west Kimberley carrying diamonds he had found in the area. It was not until 1979 that scientists finally tracked down the source of Watson's diamonds – a classic diamond 'pipe' two kilometres long and 200 metres wide. The Argyle Diamond Mine was developed at a cost of $435 million and opened in 1985.

Producing approximately five tonnes of diamonds every year, the mine also recovers more rock than any other diamond mine in the world – for every four tonnes of rock, one tonne of ore is removed to yield seven carats of diamonds. An estimated five per cent of this output is of gem quality and 45 per cent is of near gem quality; the balance is sold for industrial use.

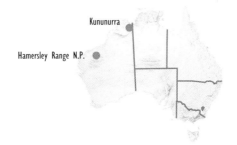

ABOVE The thorny devil is one of the reptiles that makes its home in the desert. Despite its threatening appearance, it eats only ants and termites.

LEFT Seen from the air, the lush colours of the Hamersley Range's gorges, rivers and plateaux form an almost abstract image of Western Australia's remote and ruggedly beautiful Pilbara region.

BELOW Young gums line the freshwater river where people enjoy a cooling dip at Crossing Pool, the main camping area in Millstream–Chichester National Park, 250 kilometres south-west of Port Hedland.

Kalgoorlie—Boulder

ABOVE This old hotel, the Broad Arrow Tavern near Kalgoorlie, with its deep shaded verandah and corrugated-iron roof, is typical of the welcoming pubs that appear in the middle of nowhere throughout the outback.

OPPOSITE LEFT The grand late-19th century buildings that line the main street of Kalgoorlie, including the gracious old Post Office and Telegraph Office seen here, were built from the great wealth of the gold rush era.

LEFT After the spring rains, the Western Australian desert bursts into bloom, with a carpet of wildflowers extending as far as the eye can see. The region is home to over 4000 different species of flower.

INDEX